EXERCISES FOR
MULTILINGUAL
WRITERS

THE
EVERYDAY
WRITER

EXERCISES FOR MULTILINGUAL WRITERS

THE EVERYDAY WRITER

Third Edition

Maria McCormack

COLUMBIA UNIVERSITY

BEDFORD/ST. MARTIN'S

BOSTON ◆ NEW YORK

Manufactured in the United States of America.

9 8 7 6 5
f e d c b a

For information, write: Bedford/St. Martin's, 75 Arlington Street,
Boston, MA 02116   (617-399-4000)

ISBN: 0-312-43029-9

EAN: 978-0-312-43029-0

Preface

Exercises for Multilingual Writers for *The Everyday Writer* is a resource for ESL students, writing tutors, and instructors of ESL students. Its exercises consist of sentences and paragraphs that demonstrate errors common to ESL writers. Most of them are designed so that students can edit directly on the pages of the book.

The exercise sets are numbered to correspond to chapters in Part XII of *The Everyday Writer*, "For Multilingual Writers," so that students can quickly locate help by following the cross-references in each exercise's instructions.

To help students check their own progress as they work, answers to the even-numbered exercise items appear in the back of the book. Answers to the odd-numbered exercises are given in the instructor's answer key only.

Instructors who have adopted *The Everyday Writer* as a text are welcome to photocopy any of these exercises to use for homework assignments, for classroom activities, or for quizzes. The book is also available for student purchase. Additional ESL practice exercises are available on *The Everyday Writer* Web site: <bedfordstmartins.com/everyday_writer>.

Contents

Nouns and Noun Phrases

64.1 Using count and noncount nouns

Choose the appropriate noun in each of the following sentences. (See *The Everyday Writer*, pp. 495–496.) Example:

Early immigrants to the United States often had wrong (<u>information</u>/informations) about their new country.

1. A large (number/amount) of European immigrants moved to the United States by steamboat.

2. The new immigrants had different (reason/reasons) for leaving their homeland to come to this country.

3. Many (immigrant/immigrants) came here seeking new opportunities.

4. Some sought freedom of religion, and some sought (wealth/wealths).

5. (Overpopulation/Overpopulations), famine, and disease also drove people to leave their homeland.

6. In addition, (discrimination/discriminations) by the government and police in some countries spurred emigration.

7. Immigrants to the United States have often faced (battle/battles) with current residents over jobs, housing, and the use of English.

8. (Legislation/Legislations) to discourage immigration increased in the last decade of the twentieth century.

9. For example, the Immigration Reform Act of 1995 made it clear that immigrants have to become citizens before they can qualify for Social Security (benefit/benefits).

10. Many immigrants today need the (advice/advices) of other immigrants, government officials, and social service agencies to learn what rights they have.

64.2 Revising errors in the use of count and noncount nouns

Revise each of the following sentences to correct any errors made with count and noncount nouns. (See *The Everyday Writer*, pp. 495–496.) Example:

> research
> **Recently, ~~researches~~ into American views on love showed that most**
> ^
> **young adults were looking for a soul mate.**

1. According to a recent survey by the National Marriage Project, many young people in the United States believe that they will find one special person to offer them true loves.

2. The idea that every person has a soul mate can build dangerously high expectation.

3. If people expect a perfect romance, they may end relationship that are imperfect.

4. Young adults need to be realistic when they think about the quality they want in a life partner.

5. Many marriage end because the partners have unrealistic ideas about married life.

6. A potential partner's suitabilities as a parent did not matter much to most people who took the survey.

7. Only 16 percents of the young adults surveyed believed that the main purpose of marriage was to have children.

8. The idea that a couple should have common beliefs about religions was also viewed as unimportant.

9. Is the United States becoming a nation of young romantic?

10. Perhaps too many young people are getting their informations about marriage from television and romance novels instead of from real-life examples.

64.3 Using singular and plural forms

For each of the following sentences, choose the appropriate singular or plural noun from the pair in parentheses. (See *The Everyday Writer*, p. 486.) Example:

The professor gave several (handout/<u>handouts</u>) about immigration to the class.

1. Many (immigrant/immigrants) to the United States at the turn of the twentieth century came from Europe.

2. They crossed hundreds of miles of (ocean/oceans) to escape poverty and political problems.

3. Many immigrants were fleeing from disease, which killed thousands of Europeans in many (country/countries).

4. Immigrants also came from different (corner/corners) of the world to the United States seeking their fortunes.

5. Problems drove some people away from their native countries, but others came to the United States because they wanted to own a few acres of (land/lands) or find opportunities that were unavailable at home.

6. One of the most heavily used (port/ports) of entry for immigrants to the United States was Ellis Island in New York Harbor.

7. When they arrived at Ellis Island, immigrants had to pass a number of (test/tests).

8. Anyone with symptoms of tuberculosis, smallpox, and other contagious (disease/diseases) had to return home on a departing ship.

9. Some immigrants spoke little English, and people from some cultures were also unfamiliar with the twenty-six (letter/letters) of the alphabet used in the United States.

10. Many immigration (official/officials) at Ellis Island gave these people Americanized names.

█ 64.4 █ Revising errors in the use of singular and plural forms

Revise each sentence to correct any errors in the use of singular and plural noun forms. (See *The Everyday Writer*, p. 496.) Example:

> years
> **The Beatles broke up more than thirty ~~year~~ ago.**
> ^

1. The Beatles were one of the most popular musical act of all time.

2. Four young man from Liverpool, England, made a fortune playing songs that young people everywhere loved.

3. Today, recordings by the Beatles still sell millions of copy.

4. Some buyers are middle-aged fans who have not lost any of the respects they had for the group in the 1960s.

5. They may be buying CDs since they no longer own stereo equipments that can play their old vinyl records.

6. Playing their favorite old pieces of musics may make some fans feel young again.

7. Other people buying Beatles recordings are teenager discovering the songs for the first time.

8. Even today, a teenager is likely to have heard many bits of Beatle trivias.

9. Some young listeners may become big fans, but others may not understand the fusses about the Beatles.

10. The two surviving Beatles are in their early sixties, but their fans span all age.

64.5 Identifying determiners

Underline the determiners in the following paragraph. (See *The Everyday Writer*, pp. 496–497.) The first sentence has been done for you.

Historically, Japan has not been a country that encouraged immigration. The current labor shortage, however, may force that country to start allowing immigration. Because of Japan's low birthrate, not enough new workers are entering the workforce. Then, when women do have children, few new mothers stay in the job market. In addition, Japan's population is aging faster than the population of any other developed nation. Soon, four times as many Japanese citizens will be over sixty-five as will be under that age. For these three reasons, the country will not be able to achieve economic growth or support itself unless it expands its labor pool. What strategy would have a more immediate effect than inviting immigration?

64.6 Using determiners appropriately

For each of the following sentences, choose the appropriate determiner from the pair in parentheses. "X" means "no determiner." (See *The Everyday Writer*, pp. 496–497.) Example:

Getting (X/a) good education is the most certain way to get a good job.

1. Many people decide to immigrate to the United States for their (children/children's) education.

2. Immigrant parents must also worry about finding (a/some) job to support their families.

3. There are not (many/much) good opportunities for immigrants who have no education.

4. Often, uneducated immigrants end up getting (X/a) jobs with low pay.

5. They are likely to live in (X/a) poor neighborhood.

6. In the United States, schools get some money for (they/their) budgets from taxes paid in the area.

7. (Many/Much) schools in poor neighborhoods do not have enough money to pay teachers well or provide good facilities for students.

8. Unfortunately, (X/a) student from a poor neighborhood may have to be exceptionally motivated to get a decent education.

9. (Every/All) children should have an equal opportunity to be educated and find fulfilling work.

10. Perhaps someday (X/this) ideal will become a reality for all of (America/America's) children.

64.7   Revising errors in the use of determiners

Each of the following sentences contains a determiner error. Revise each sentence, adding, deleting, and changing determiners wherever appropriate. (See *The Everyday Writer*, pp. 496–497.) Example:

Millions of Americans are afraid to speak in front of ^a^ group.

1. Much businesses today expect executives to be good public speakers.

2. In fact, person who cannot speak well in public is unlikely to be promoted to an executive position.

3. However, 40 percent of all Americans have terrible fear of public speaking.

4. For these people, giving some speech is usually a miserable experience.

5. Experts suggest a little ways to help conquer a fear of public speaking.

6. Taking few deep breaths before a speech gives the speaker extra oxygen and can calm nerves.

7. Some speakers feel more confident when they imagine the audience in they underwear.

8. When speakers remember something that made them laugh recently, funny memory can help them to relax.

9. People who have an extreme problems with public speaking might need professional help.

10. Many organizations can help to conquer a businessperson fear of giving speeches.

64.8　Using articles appropriately

For each of the following sentences, choose the appropriate article from the words in parentheses. "X" means "no article." (See *The Everyday Writer*, pp. 497–499.) Example:

(A/An/The/X) love of two people can transcend cultural differences.

1. (A/An/The/X) marriage that unites people from different cultures can be very difficult.

2. However, it is often (a/an/the/X) easiest way to build a relationship with someone from a different culture.

3. After all, (a/an/the/X) love makes people willing to try to appreciate new things.

4. But people usually have to overcome several obstacles if they consider marrying (a/an/the/X) person from another culture.

5. In some cultures, people believe that men should have (a/an/the/X) main role in supporting a family.

6. A man from one of these cultures might be unhappy with (a/an/the/X) working wife, especially one who earns more than he does.

7. In certain cultures, (a/an/the/X) wives are even considered the property of their husband's family.

8. (A/An/The/X) woman who would be unable to live happily in a male-dominated household should avoid marrying a traditional man from such a culture.

9. Some people develop (a/an/the/X) interest in their beloved's culture that is so strong that they are willing to leave their own traditions behind.

10. However, many of the happiest cross-cultural marriages are those in which the couple finds (a/an/the/X) appropriate balance between their traditions.

64.9   Eliminating unnecessary articles

In each of the following sentences, eliminate the italicized article if it is unnecessary or incorrect. If the italicized article is necessary, write C. (See *The Everyday Writer*, pp. 497–499.) Example:

> Many
> ~~The many~~ Americans disagree about prayer in public schools.
>   ^

1. Freedom of *a* religion is guaranteed to all residents of the United States by the country's constitution.

2. The United States does not have *an* established state religion.

3. Instead, by *the* law, all residents are allowed to worship as they please or to choose not to worship at all.

4. The U.S. Supreme Court declared *the* school prayer unconstitutional about forty years ago.

5. Some Americans are still not certain what *the* members of the court outlawed in their ruling.

6. Students in *an* American public school are not forbidden to pray silently in class—for example, before a test.

7. Student religious organizations can meet before *a* school starts.

8. However, teachers or *the* other authority figures in a school may not legally lead prayers in class or at school functions.

9. The U.S. Constitution does not restrict the practice of *the* personal religious beliefs.

10. But, the law does not permit the use of *a* class time in public schools for group expression of a particular faith.

64.10 Revising errors in the use of articles

Revise each of the following sentences, adding, deleting, and changing articles wherever necessary. (See *The Everyday Writer*, pp. 497–499.) Example:

The
Hispanic population of the United States is growing faster than any
^
other minority group.

1. Politicians in the most states now realize the importance of trying to win the Hispanic vote.

2. Grouping all Hispanics together ignores a fact that Hispanic Americans come from many different countries and cultures.

3. Cultures of Cuba and Mexico are different, just as the cultures of France and Sweden are different.

4. Just as not every Irish American agrees on political issues, there is not the single issue that guarantees all Hispanics' approval.

5. Some issues may capture an interest of the majority of Hispanic American voters, however.

6. A high percentage of Hispanic residents of the United States believe that governments should provide assistance to a poor.

7. Government help to reduce poverty is usually considered the liberal position.

8. However, many Hispanic Americans are in the agreement with conservative political opinions about social issues.

9. In 2001, George W. Bush became a first U.S. president to broadcast a speech in Spanish to appeal to Hispanic American voters.

10. His tactic may or may not have had the effect on Hispanic approval of his positions, for Hispanics in this country also disagree about the politics of speaking Spanish.

64.11 Arranging modifiers appropriately

Revise each of the following sentences to correct any errors in the arrangement of modifiers. (See *The Everyday Writer*, pp. 499–500.) Example:

> chemical problem
> **Attention deficit disorder, or A.D.D., results from a ~~problem chemical~~**
> **in the brain.**

1. Most people with attention deficit disorder display behavioral obvious symptoms such as hyperactivity, disorganization, impulsiveness, and an inability to manage time effectively.

2. These all symptoms affect performance in certain jobs.

3. A.D.D. was once thought to exist only in children, but now in this field experts believe that adults can also suffer from it.

4. Nowadays, new research and openness about the condition help prevent job potential discrimination.

5. Most adults would have trouble remaining completely focused on a thirty-minute boring slide presentation.

6. For an adult with A.D.D., such a task is a cognitive huge burden.

7. Modifications simple in the work routine can help A.D.D. sufferers be more effective.

8. Organizing paperwork by color and size clears up kinds of some confusion for A.D.D. sufferers.

9. For example, a green large folder might contain invoices, and a small blue folder could hold receipts.

10. If it is not possible for them to change office daily confusing routines, A.D.D. sufferers should consider changing careers.

Verbs and Verb Phrases

65.1   Using verb phrases

For each of the following sentences, choose the appropriate verb form from the pair in parentheses. (See *The Everyday Writer*, pp. 501–503.) Example:

In California, hundreds of millions of dollars (spent/<u>are spent</u>)

annually to provide bilingual education to students with limited

proficiency in English.

1. Bilingual education programs are (regard/regarded) as a failure by many Americans.

2. Many graduates of these programs have not (learn/learned) good English skills.

3. The United States would (face/facing) a serious problem if citizens expected the government alone to meet every need.

4. Some states (are trying/trying) to eliminate bilingual education classes in their schools.

5. Bilingual programs have not usually (ask/asked) parents and community groups for input.

6. Parents must (involve/to involve) themselves in bilingual programs.

7. Parents who have time should (volunteer/volunteering) with community organizations to propel bilingual education forward.

8. Many people (believe/are believing) that this kind of activism would enable bilingual education to reach its goal.

9. A student could (achieve/achieves) fluency in English with the help of his or her parents.

10. In order to overcome discrimination, citizens must be (unite/united) to solve the language problem.

65.2 Revising verb phrases

Each of the following sentences contains a verb phrase error. Revise each sentence. (See *The Everyday Writer*, pp. 501–503.) Example:

Many people who ~~are~~ study English as a foreign language focus on learning the grammar of written English.

1. Students of English are often surprise by the differences between written and conversational English.

2. Those students who have study formal written English may find conversational English difficult to understand.

3. Students who have recently came to an English-speaking country may have particular trouble with slang vocabulary and expressions.

4. Conversation classes in English supposed to help students become familiar with spoken English by simulating real-life situational dialogues.

5. Students who have not exposed to spoken English can listen to English radio or TV broadcasts to help them learn English.

6. Just listening to spoken English can useful in learning oral speech patterns and intonation.

7. Many students find that listening to songs with English lyrics can helps them learn new vocabulary and expressions.

8. Some students who do not feeling a need to learn spoken English might prefer to listen to radio broadcasts in their native language rather than broadcasts in English.

9. If such students do not make a great effort to learn conversational English, they may never can understand the spoken language well.

10. Students in English classes who may not have working hard on learning spoken English need to understand that an inability to speak and understand English can limit their opportunities.

65.3 Making subjects and verbs agree

In each of the following sentences, circle the subject, and then choose the correct verb from the pair in parentheses to establish subject-verb agreement. (See *The Everyday Writer*, pp. 501–503.) Example:

The high (cost) of rescuing careless visitors (<u>is</u>/are) probably the reason why many national parks have been adopting stricter safety guide-lines lately.

1. One of the national parks' greatest problems in recent years (has/have) been the number of visitors who require rescue missions.

2. A man and his nine-year-old daughter (was/were) posing next to a bison at Yellowstone when the bison butted the girl, according to a park spokesperson.

3. Several visitors at Yellowstone's geothermal pools (has/have) died because they left the marked paths, strayed too close to the boiling pools, and fell in.

4. Each of these examples (shows/show) that people take excessive risks in parks.

5. The biggest cause of emergencies (is/are) heat exhaustion.

6. The two ideas emphasized in the Grand Canyon's current safety campaign (is/are) that people should eat and drink regularly while on the trails and that they should avoid hiking during the heat of the day.

7. A parent or hike leader sometimes (put/puts) the members of a hiking party in danger, but anyone who ignores basic safety measures can be fined or even jailed.

8. Nevada's Lake Mead Recreation Area is one of the many national parks that (is/are) banning alcohol in order to reduce risky behavior on the part of visitors.

9. There (is/are) several reasons why people take safety risks in parks.

10. The desire for good photographs (is/are) one of the main reasons people forget to be cautious.

65.4 Using the present and past tenses

For each of the following sentences, choose the appropriate verb from the pair in parentheses. (See *The Everyday Writer*, pp. 503–504.) Example:

When I first came to the United States, I (can/<u>could</u>) speak only a few words of English.

1. When I came to this country, I (go/went) to a huge school.

2. I (remember/remembered) that my fourth-grade teachers used to give me books of pictures and alphabet letters.

3. Before long, however, I (become/became) very good at reading.

4. When my family made me return to my native country, I (am/was) so depressed that I didn't leave the house for weeks.

5. They told me, "You (have to/had to) go to school."

6. Three years later, history (repeats/repeated) itself, and my family returned to the United States.

7. I told my American friends that I (am/was) glad to be back.

8. Two years later, I (graduate/graduated) from high school with a 3.87 GPA.

9. The following fall I (start/started) college.

10. Now I (take/took) courses in business and computer programming to prepare for a career.

65.5 Revising errors in the present and past tenses

In each of the following sentences, change the italicized verb to the appropriate tense. (See *The Everyday Writer*, pp. 503–504.) Example:

began

Several years ago, many states *begin* administering standardized tests

in public schools.

1. In 1995, my eighth-grade teacher told us we *have* to take our state's math and reading tests at the end of the school year.

2. My teacher *spends* the whole spring of 1996 drilling us on the practice tests.

3. School officials came to our class and announced that students *cannot* pass or fail the test.

4. Instead, they said that our school and the teachers *are* being tested.

5. The students agreed that nobody *is* fooled by the officials' remarks.

6. My friend Hector said, "The test results *were* going to be sent to our parents."

7. In May of that year, we *sit* in class every day for a week completing the test.

8. I *score* in the fiftieth percentile, so my results were exactly average.

9. Now I think of those results and *remembered* the eighth grade fondly.

10. I still believe that kids *learned* more in school when less time is spent on test preparation.

65.6 Using simple, perfect, and progressive verb phrases

For each of the following sentences, choose the appropriate verb phrase from the pair in parentheses. (See *The Everyday Writer*, pp. 504–505.) Example:

In the past ten years, bottled water (became/has become) increasingly popular in America.

While I (shopped/was shopping) at a grocery store last week, I (counted/was counting) five different brands of bottled water on the shelves. These days, bottled water (costs/is costing) more than carbonated beverages, but many consumers now (feel/are feeling) that good health is worth the greater price.

Nutrition experts (have observed/have been observing) that Americans (consume/have consumed) too much soda and junk food. Prior to these findings, some parents (noticed/have noticed) that their children were more sluggish and inattentive after they (had eaten/were eating) junk food. In many cases they (had been snacking/have been snacking) at school.

Now nutrition experts insist that children (need/are needing) breakfast before school so that they (do not stop/have not been stopping) at vending machines for sodas or greasy snacks. Because studies (showed/have shown) that students perform better when they eat nutritious foods, some schools (consider/are considering) a ban on certain junk foods and soda machines. However, many parents (believe/are believing) that good nutrition should be enforced by parents, not schools. They (resent/are resenting) being told by the school administration what not to put in their child's lunch. Based on recent sales of bottled water, it (appears/is appearing) that consumers (make/are making) better nutritional choices.

65.7 Revising simple, perfect, and progressive verb phrases

Revise each of the following sentences by correcting errors in verb phrases, using simple, perfect, and progressive verb forms where appropriate. (See *The Everyday Writer*, pp. 504–505.) Example:

> **In 1954, the U.S. Supreme Court ~~has~~ desegregated education, declaring that "separate educational facilities are inherently unequal."**

1. Since then, the states often challenged the federal government either by ignoring or refusing to implement the decision or by filing court cases.

2. The case of Central High School in Little Rock, Arkansas, has been one of the most famous examples of a state fighting this federal mandate.

3. When the school has opened in September 1957, the Arkansas National Guard was called out to prevent African Americans from entering the school.

4. President Dwight D. Eisenhower ordered the army into Little Rock to enforce the court order, and African American children finally were entering the school with the protection of federal troops.

5. State-supported resistance to desegregation was not ending with the Little Rock case.

6. However, over the years the courts consistently ruled in favor of desegregation.

7. Racial integration of schools is remaining a concern for the current generation as well.

8. Recent statistics are showing that about 35 percent of African American students go to schools in which 90 percent of the student body is nonwhite.

9. In addition, support for integration declines in the current political climate.

10. Today, the fight for desegregation was largely replaced by the fight for quality education for all students.

65.8 Using modals appropriately

For each of the following sentences, choose the appropriate modal from the pair in parentheses. (See *The Everyday Writer*, pp. 506–507.) Example:

Fifty years ago, most people (cannot/<u>could not</u>) learn to use computers.

1. Today, few Americans (will/would) consider living without the conveniences they take for granted.

2. People in the United States (can/could) perform many daily tasks easily because tools to simplify life are widely available.

3. Financial tasks are one example of chores that (will/would) have been more difficult in the years before home computers.

4. Now, Americans (can/could) use computers to view their accounts and pay their bills.

5. With the right computer software, ordinary people (may/might) do their own taxes rather than hire accountants or try to understand the fine print in tax forms themselves.

6. Software today knows more about current tax law than most people do, and software of all types (should/would) continue to become more sophisticated.

7. Household chores (can/could) also take more time if Americans did not have appliances made more efficient by technology.

8. What modern kitchen (will/would) be complete without an automatic dishwasher?

9. Washing dishes by hand (would/should) take more human effort than loading a dishwasher, and filling a sink to wash dishes (might/may) even use more water than running the machine.

10. (Would/Will) Americans ever miss doing chores the old-fashioned way?

65.9   Revising errors in modal use

Revise each of the following sentences to correct errors in the use of modals. (See *The Everyday Writer*, pp. 506–507.) Example:

> **Before I enrolled at the university, I thought that getting any kind of**
> **degree w̶i̶l̶l̶ help me get a job.**
> *would*

1. I soon discovered that I must choose a major after two years of coursework.

2. I cannot decide what career field interested me most, so selecting a major was difficult.

3. At the beginning of my third year of coursework, I must make a choice.

4. My adviser told me that I can change my mind later if I decided I wasn't happy with my decision.

5. I decided that I will study engineering.

6. When I took my first engineering course, I discovered that I can't understand some of the math required to complete my homework assignments.

7. I realized that I would have taken more advanced math courses to prepare for my engineering classes.

8. Now I am taking an extra math course to catch up, and I would finish my engineering degree next spring.

9. I couldn't wait until I start work as an engineer.

10. In the meantime, my professors tell me that I would study diligently to prepare for my career.

65.10 Choosing appropriate modals

For each of the following sentences, fill in the blank with an appropriate modal and the correct form of the verb in parentheses. More than one answer may be correct. (See *The Everyday Writer*, pp. 506–507.) Example:

People who are considering travel outside their native country

<u>should learn</u> **(learn) about the culture and language of the country**

they plan to visit.

1. If I had planned the time before my trip more carefully, I

_____ (study) the language and culture before traveling.

2. In my first few weeks out of my own country, I _____

(struggle) to communicate in all my interactions with people.

3. I _____ (consider) returning to my native country immediately, but I knew I would regret it later.

4. If I hadn't been so curious about the country I was visiting, I _____ (stay) in my apartment.

5. But, in order to make the most of my time away from home, I knew I _____ (venture) out on my own and face the language barrier.

6. Now, after living here for more than a year, I _____ (enjoy) the culture much more, because I have learned the language well.

7. In fact, I _____ (have) a difficult time readjusting to my native environment if I returned.

8. I am afraid that I _____ (feel) the same alienation in my native country if I returned home now that I felt when I first arrived in this country.

9. Besides, I _____ (miss) my new friends if I left this country.

10. When my family comes to visit me here, I _____ (prepare) them for the many cultural differences I encountered here over a year ago.

65.11   Using participial adjectives

For each of the following sentences, choose the appropriate participial adjective from the pair in parentheses. (See *The Everyday Writer*, p. 507.) Example:

One of the most (fascinated/<u>fascinating</u>) recent developments in medicine is the use of robots in surgery.

1. Many doctors are (excited/exciting) about the advantages robots have over humans in medicine.

2. Of course, a robot will never be able to calm a nervous patient with a (soothed/soothing) explanation of a medical procedure.

3. A (terrified/terrifying) patient about to undergo surgery might prefer a human doctor.

4. However, robot "surgeons" never become (tired/tiring) when standing for hours during an operation.

5. Of course, an (observed/observing) doctor will control the robot's actions.

6. Surgical robots can correct the movements of a doctor's (shaken/shaking) hands.

7. These robots, equipped with cameras, magnifying lenses, and bright lights, allow doctors an (amazed/amazing) view inside the human body without the need for large incisions.

8. Robotic surgical assistance should decrease the number of (horrified/horrifying) problems that can happen during and after surgery because of human errors.

9. Instead, the robots and their human operators can complete surgery with more (satisfied/satisfying) results.

10. Someday, surgical patients may be (surprised/surprising) to learn that their doctor had mechanical assistance during the operation.

65.12 Revising errors in the use of participial adjectives

Revise any of the following sentences that do not use participial adjectives correctly. If a sentence does not contain an error, write C. (See *The Everyday Writer*, p. 507.) Example:

astonished
The ~~astonishing~~ medical students could hardly believe the realism of
 ^
their new mechanical practice patient.

1. Suffered patients have been used for medical students' practice in teaching hospitals for decades.

2. No matter how interested a student is in medical school lectures, the lectures cannot prepare him or her to perform procedures on patients.

3. Sitting in a packing lecture hall, first- and second-year medical students can only imagine working on a real patient.

4. However, disgusting patients soon tire of having amateurs use them to practice starting IVs, drawing blood, and giving injections.

5. Repeated practice is absolutely necessary for good medical technique, but what patients are willing to let medical students spend hours prodding and poking them?

6. New technologically advanced fiberglass "patients" allow fumbling medical students to practice on them for as long as the students wish.

7. A distressing medical student may choke a mechanical patient repeatedly while trying to put a tube down its throat, and the machine will utter a loud gagging noise.

8. The gagging sound is unnerved, but students' mistakes do not hurt any living human beings.

9. The uncomplained mechanical patients allow students to develop good medical technique before they handle real people.

10. When these teaching techniques become more widespread, hospitalized people all over the United States will be relieving.

Prepositions and Prepositional Phrases

66.1 Using prepositions appropriately

For each of the following sentences, choose the appropriate preposition from the pair in parentheses. "X" means "no preposition." (See *The Everyday Writer*, pp. 508–509.) Example:

Most (X/of) teenagers in the United States work part-time jobs

during the school year.

1. Teenagers want to show (X/to) people that they can stand on their own two feet.

2. Because they crave independence, teenagers don't want their families taking care (to/of) them financially.

3. Many adults don't agree (to/with) this idea; they believe that working diminishes precious study time.

4. Not only can working interfere (in/with) schoolwork, but it can also negatively affect teenagers' health.

5. When I was (in/at) high school, my best friend, an excellent student, took a part-time job.

6. She thought she could handle both work and school, but (in/on) fact, she did not have enough time to do her homework.

7. Her grade-point average fell (on/from) 3.95 (to/on) 2.40.

8. Her parents finally objected (to/on) the amount of time she spent at work.

9. The choices teenagers make (in/at) these years will affect the rest of their lives.

10. Teenagers are sometimes confused (on/about) their priorities: are they first and foremost students or workers?

66.2 Revising inappropriate prepositions

Revise each of the following sentences so that prepositions are used correctly. (See *The Everyday Writer*, pp. 508–509.) Example:

Some people argue that work has a positive influence ~~in~~ teenagers.

(on)

1. Some parents don't make any effort to understand to teenagers.

2. At such situations, the workplace can provide a place for teens to interact with adult role models.

3. At work, teenagers can learn to form relationships between other people.

4. While they are in high school, students spend a lot of time to their friends or in class.

5. Work, in the other hand, often requires teenagers to cooperate with people they may not know or like very well.

6. Working also gives students something to do at the hours after school.

7. Teenagers with nothing to do after school are more likely to get at trouble.

8. A part-time job can allow teens to pay leisure activities that they would otherwise be unable to afford.

9. Having a little money to spend in things they want or need makes teenagers feel more independent.

10. A teenager's ability to succeed both as a student and as a worker

    depends largely in his or her sense of responsibility.

66.3 Using two-word verbs

For each of the following sentences, choose the appropriate word from the pair in parentheses to complete the sentence. (See *The Everyday Writer*, pp. 508–511.)

I'd agree (to/<u>with</u>) anyone who said that college life is a big adjustment.

1. On my first day at college, I was approached (with/by) a student who asked me for directions.

2. I inferred (from/in) his question that he was a first-year student and new to the campus.

3. I empathized (for/with) his situation: the campus was very large and all the buildings looked the same to me.

4. I was also adapting (with/to) college life.

5. I responded (by/with) giving him the directions he'd asked for.

6. Then I suggested that he look (on/at) the campus map located near the library.

7. After he set (up/off) for the library, I went to the student union for more information about campus activities.

8. While walking around the student union, I heard some students allude (on/to) all the late nights they spent studying.

9. One student in particular had to report (on/for) an experiment she had conducted in her lab course.

10. I wondered how I would adjust (with/to) the workload as well as the unfamiliar environment of the university.

66.4 Revising errors in the use of two-word verbs

Each of the following sentences contains an error in the use of two-word verbs. Revise each sentence. (See *The Everyday Writer*, pp. 508–511.) Example:

Because I was apprehensive about my first day of class, I slipped
into
~~onto~~ a chair in the back of the classroom.
^

1. The professor walked into the room and began to elaborate over her course requirements.

2. I looked around the course syllabus while she talked.

3. She went on to say that she did not discriminate towards students in any way; she was interested only in the quality of their work.

4. Neither would she cater for the whims of individual students, she added.

5. She warned us not to try to negotiate against her regarding our grades.

6. She then turned on her discussion of the syllabus to tell an anecdote from her teaching experiences.

7. Returning to the course syllabus, she impressed in us the value of appropriate preparation for each class.

8. She further encouraged us to invest on our education by developing good study habits for all our classes.

9. Just before class ended, she asked if we had any questions pertaining about the course.

10. I concluded of her discussion that she wanted to be sure students would take her class seriously.

Clauses and Sentences

67.1 Choosing appropriate subjects

For each of the following sentences, choose the appropriate subject from the words in parentheses. "X" means "no subject necessary." (See *The Everyday Writer*, pp. 511–512.) Example:

(It/There/X) is much difference of opinion in the United States about the effects of television on young viewers.

1. Television (it/there/X) is available to almost everyone in the United States.

2. (It/There/X) is almost impossible to avoid television in some public places.

3. Some people believe that (it/there/X) is important for television programs to be constructive.

4. In particular, they argue that (it/there/X) is essential for children to receive positive messages from television.

5. (It/There/X) is much popular support for the idea that violent television shows can harm young viewers.

6. However, (it/there/X) is also true that many adults enjoy violent or graphic programs.

7. Many Americans believe that the media (it/there/X) is not to blame for how we use the information presented.

8. (It/There/X) are ways for individuals to use media information wisely, many people say.

9. Many Americans argue that (it/there/X) is up to parents or guardians to make sure that children do not watch inappropriate television shows.

10. Most Americans seem to feel that (it/there/X) should not be government censorship of television programs.

67.2 Revising for appropriate verb placement

Revise each of the following sentences so that the verb is in the appropriate position. (See *The Everyday Writer*, pp. 512–513.) Example:

Most Americans government censorship. don't want

1. Many people that too much sex and violence is shown on television believe.

2. Like most parents would to monitor their children's television viewing.

3. For many people, however, keeping track of a child's choice of television programs impossible is.

4. One solution might from recent technological innovations come.

5. Several years ago, agreed American television manufacturers to start equipping all new televisions with a V-chip.

6. The *V* for "violence" stands.

7. The V-chip out screens shows that contain sex and violence.

8. Parents the chip program to block shows with certain ratings.

9. With the V-chip, censor individuals, not the government, their children's television programs.

10. Of course, today, many children better than their parents know how to program electronic devices.

67.3 Revising for English word order

Revise each of the following sentences so that subjects, verbs, and objects are in the correct English word order. (See *The Everyday Writer*, pp. 512–513.) Example:

Are (there) several problems with the V-chip system.

1. The television industry ratings for television programs provides so that parents can decide what to allow their children to watch.

2. The ratings system similar is to the one used for movies.

3. The ratings system exists already, but people get a V-chip only when they a new television buy.

4. Older children might to programming rated as explicit be attracted.

5. Most parents know that want kids what they are not allowed to have.

6. Parents with an older television shows rated for mature audiences will not be able to block out.

7. Say some critics that it is only a matter of time before a child learns to tamper with the V-chip programmer.

8. Advertisers worry that parents will block out the prime-time shows that the most advertising revenue generate.

9. If a show an explicit rating has, parents might block it out and advertisers might shy away.

10. The television industry argues that the V-chip a kind of censorship is since it will indirectly control the kinds of shows produced.

67.4 Identifying noun clauses

Underline the noun clause in each of the following sentences, and
identify it as a subject or object clause in the sentence. (See *The Everyday Writer*, p. 513.) Example:

> **U.S. companies in the global economy feel <u>that they must send an</u>**
>
> **<u>increasing number of executives abroad.</u>** *object clause*

1. Many companies sending executives abroad believe that their most
   difficult challenge will be helping their employees deal with culture
   shock in a foreign environment.

2. How companies can help executives to cope when they return is an
   even more serious problem.

3. Recent research proves that these professionals are unsatisfied with the
   way their companies are handling their repatriation.

4. A study reveals that 25 percent of returning employees leave their
   companies within a year.

5. Whatever investment the company made in the employee is lost when
   the employee leaves.

6. That so much money is at stake motivates top managers to investigate
   the reasons for employee dissatisfaction.

7. Many people wonder whether much employee dissatisfaction stems
   from poor planning by the company.

8. Many returning executives complain that their companies didn't tell
   them exactly what they would be working on when they returned.

9. A majority of returnees are unable to use the experience they
   gained abroad, which demonstrates that companies are not thinking
   ahead.

10. How companies will address these repatriation issues is a challenge for today's business world.

67.5 Using noun clauses

Revise each of the following sentences by moving the noun clause to the end of the sentence and, if necessary, adding a dummy subject. (See *The Everyday Writer*, p. 513.) Example:

That airlines limit the amount of carry-on baggage has always frustrated business travelers.

It has always frustrated business travelers that airlines limit the amount of carry-on baggage.

1. Why passengers can only bring two pieces of luggage into the airplane cabin is rarely discussed by the airline industry.

2. That these two pieces not exceed certain size requirements is mandatory.

3. That travelers couldn't fit everything they needed for a business trip into these small bags was often the case.

4. Whichever bags exceeded size restrictions had to be handed over by travelers as checked luggage.

5. That the airlines often lost checked baggage irritated many passengers.

6. In addition, whenever checked bags took a long time to arrive at the baggage claim often upset busy business travelers' schedules.

7. That the airlines have been looking for solutions to this problem is encouraging.

8. That airplanes should increase the amount of space available in overhead bins so that passengers can bring more and larger carry-ons has been suggested by major airlines.

9. That airplanes can achieve departure six to eight minutes faster with the larger bins has been shown by recent studies.

10. Whether flight attendants will be happy about this change is uncertain.

67.6   Revising errors in noun clauses

Revise each of the following sentences to correct any errors made with noun clauses. (See *The Everyday Writer*, p. 513.) Example:

That their computer systems are crashing companies would like to discover the reason.

Companies would like to discover the reason that their computer systems are crashing.

1. Is evident why some companies are becoming concerned about what their employees are doing.

2. The amount of email that employees send and receive each day systems administrators can use software to see.

3. Is necessary for the company to know that an employee emails jokes from a business computer?

4. Could be considered a breach of privacy when managers read employees' email.

5. One employee said that would sue her company for breach of privacy.

6. The systems administrator tells employees that is his job to prevent problems.

7. That cause managers to install monitoring software there are many reasons.

8. Is true that companies have to buy more bandwidth if their employees send huge amounts of email.

9. Whenever their email is scrutinized but senior executives' email is not lower-level employees are concerned.

10. Is important that managers create an atmosphere that makes employees feel trusted and fairly treated.

67.7 Using infinitives and gerunds

For each sentence in the following paragraph, choose either the infinitive or the gerund in parentheses. (See *The Everyday Writer*, pp. 514–515.) Example:

Anyone who plans (to study/studying) in another country should be aware that university systems differ from place to place.

Since a university education in one country may differ from a university experience in another, students studying outside their native country may struggle (to understand/understanding) educational attitudes within foreign institutions. For example, in some countries, students are expected (to avoid/avoiding) (to speak/speaking) in class, but in other countries it is expected, if not required. Moreover, instructors in some countries encourage students (to participate/participating) actively by (to solve/solving) problems in groups, (to make/making) presentations, and (to examine/examining) case studies.

Another aspect of the foreign classroom that is often confusing is the teacher-student relationship. In many countries this relationship is a formal one; in other countries it can appear (to be/being) more relaxed. Regardless of the level of formality between teacher and student, students should remember (to meet/meeting) deadlines for assignments and (to treat/treating) the professor with respect. Even if a professor meets with students outside of class (to have/having) coffee with them, this shouldn't make the professor appear (to be/being) any less of an authority figure.

67.8 Using infinitives and gerunds appropriately

For each of the following sentences, fill in the blank with the appropriate infinitive or gerund formed from the verb in parentheses. (See *The Everyday Writer*, pp. 514–515.) Example:

It is easy to understand foreign students' _____being_____ (be) confused about grades in American university classes.

1. Most U.S. professors prefer their students _____ (work) independently, but professors do offer help to students who need it.

2. University policies forbid students _____ (share) answers on a test.

3. However, instructors often encourage their students _____ (collaborate) in teams on projects other than tests and papers.

4. Universities consider _____ (plagiarize) written work as grounds for expulsion.

5. Dishonest students may jeopardize their relationship with other students who resent their _____ (cheat).

6. Instructors expect students _____ (do) the work for a class even if the work is not graded.

7. Some teachers believe that not grading an assignment enables students _____ (judge) their own work.

8. If students want to improve their grades, professors often support students' _____ (work) with a tutor.

9. But most professors don't appreciate their students' _____ (ask) about grades on a test or paper in the middle of class.

10. Students who want class time to discuss grades risk _____ (anger) their professors.

67.9 Revising errors in infinitives and gerunds

Revise each sentence to correct any errors in the use of infinitives and gerunds. (See *The Everyday Writer*, pp. 514–515.) Example:

Understanding the nature of competition in an American university
                                           to succeed
is necessary for students ~~succeeding~~ **there.**
                                           ^

1. International students who are considering to study in the United States should realize that relationships between students here can be either cooperative or competitive, depending on the class.

2. International students who expect cooperating with classmates may initially feel uncomfortable with the competition in American schools.

3. Of course, they should not hesitate asking their classmates for help.

4. In some courses, however, the instructor might decide calculating students' grades in relation to one another.

5. This method of to grade is called a curve.

6. When a curve is used, students may be reluctant sharing their lecture notes with others because they don't want to hurt their own grades.

7. Students without high grade-point averages risk not to get into a top graduate program.

8. Employers trying to fill a job opening may also choose looking at a candidate's grade-point average and faculty recommendations.

9. When students under pressure are asked deciding between helping classmates and decreasing competition for a high grade-point average, they often choose the latter.

10. International students sometimes have to get used to function in this competitive system.

67.10   Forming adjective clauses

Combine each pair of sentences into a single sentence containing an adjective clause. (See *The Everyday Writer*, pp. 515–517.) Example:

Teenagers are getting plastic surgery. The number of them is rising.

The number of teenagers who are getting plastic surgery is rising.

1. I spoke to a surgeon. He said that plastic surgery is sometimes a parent's idea rather than a teen's.

2. However, more often the teenager is the one. He or she convinces the parent to pay for procedures.

3. High school can be a harsh environment. The slightest physical imperfections can provoke torment and teasing.

4. Media images of young men and women show impossibly perfect faces and bodies. Teens are frequently exposed to these images.

5. Like it or not, we are living in a superficial culture. Attractive people get better treatment than unattractive people.

6. Therefore, people are requesting plastic surgery. Their bodies aren't even fully developed.

7. One woman was insistent about changing her appearance. She went to a plastic surgeon's office.

8. She demanded to have the wrinkles removed. The wrinkles were around her eyes.

9. There were just two problems. The surgeon pointed out these problems to her.

10. The problems were that she was nineteen and that she had no wrinkles. The problems prevented her from having the surgery.

67.11 Revising errors in the use of relative pronouns in adjective clauses

In each of the following sentences, underline the relative pronoun in the adjective clause. Then, revise the sentence, removing the relative pronoun from the adjective clause wherever possible. If the sentence is correct with the relative pronoun in place, write C. (See *The Everyday Writer*, pp. 515–517.) Examples:

> The permanent visual statement <u>that</u> is made by a tattoo is popular with many people today.
>
> *The permanent visual statement made by a tattoo is popular with many people today.*
>
> Despite the popularity of tattoos, some people who have them want them removed. *C*

1. Sometimes tattoos, which are status symbols in certain groups, tend to blur over time and lose their appeal.

2. For example, a tattoo of a red rose that has faded to a brown blob is no longer attractive.

3. When some people change careers or leave a particular group, they say that they want their tattoos removed.

4. For instance, a musician with tattoos might not stand out, but a dentist with tattoos might be someone whom patients become nervous about.

5. Also, some tattoo wearers need to remove tattoos that they got years earlier with a former girlfriend's or boyfriend's name.

6. Removing a tattoo with which one no longer feels comfortable is sometimes just a sign of moving on to a new stage in life.

7. One man whose son was nine years old was getting a tattoo removed because he didn't want his son to think tattoos were cool.

8. Each treatment to remove tattoos, which is done by laser, costs four to six hundred dollars.

9. For a tattoo that has especially stubborn dye, several treatments may be needed.

10. The old method of removing tattoos, which entailed basically grinding it off, left scars, but the laser treatment does not.

67.12 Revising errors in adjective clauses

Revise the following paragraph to correct the errors in adjective clauses. (See *The Everyday Writer*, pp. 515–517.) Example:

For people ~~which~~ who are considering plastic surgery, there is a new way to prepare for the procedure.

Nowadays, there are several Internet sites that they show live broadcasts of cosmetic surgery. If people miss the live coverage, they can pull up archival video footage in that patients undergo procedures from liposuction to facelifts. This new trend shows that plastic surgery has gone from something was considered shameful or vain to something is considered normal or even a status symbol. The ten million Americans who had plastic surgery in the 1990s represent every social stratum. Moreover, the majority of Americans whose had plastic surgery came from households that they earned below $60,000. The popularity of the Web casts also demonstrates how much people love to watch live procedures which there is a lot of blood and gore. How do patients feel about being the subject of broadcasts in that their bodies are sliced open? Apparently, just fine; the procedures, are free for online patients, attract hundreds of emails per day from candidates.

67.13 Selecting appropriate verb forms in conditional sentences

Choose the appropriate verb form from the pair in parentheses for each of the following sentences. (See *The Everyday Writer*, pp. 517–518.) Example:

If an instructor asks that her students (are/<u>be</u>) prepared to discuss a book for class, should they be allowed to watch a "book-to-movie" adaptation prior to the class discussion?

1. Some instructors say that if students (had/will have) access to film versions of the reading assignments, they would neglect to do the reading.

2. An instructor may insist that students (not watch/will not watch) a film version if the class discussion of the reading material has not yet taken place.

3. If another instructor (is/were) asked, he might say that watching the film, when done in conjunction with the assigned reading, would enhance the students' learning experience.

4. Such instructors maintain that if students (are/were) to watch only the film version, the quality of their comments would reveal that they had not read the book.

5. Even if students watched a film version of an assigned book, the film by no means (would take/will take) the place of reading the book.

6. Also, students may feel that their learning experiences are being limited if they (are/were) not permitted to watch the film version.

7. Some educators are afraid that if a film adaptation of every book (is/were) to exist, students would quit reading books altogether.

8. If students (turn/had turned) to visual media instead of reading their assigned texts, educators feel that the importance of reading will be minimized.

9. A few instructors may even feel that if completion of reading assignments (isn't/wasn't) enforced, film as a medium will supplant literary texts.

10. If film (had become/becomes) the preferred medium for the

transmission of ideas, will books become obsolete?

67.14 Using appropriate verb forms in conditional sentences

In the following paragraphs, fill in the blanks with the appropriate form of the verb in parentheses. Modals may be used, and more than one answer may be correct. (See *The Everyday Writer*, pp. 517–518.) Example:

If people really (want) _____ wanted _____ to protect their privacy, they

would be less willing to give information to stores and Web sites.

(1) If a company (want) _____ personal information about

its customers badly enough to pay for it, should customers give up their pri-

vacy for discounts? (2) A drugstore chain in my neighborhood has begun to

offer a discount card; if customers have this card, they (receive)

_____ substantial discounts on purchases. (3) The discounts

(appear) _____ when the card is swiped if the customer has

purchased selected products. (4) However, customers have to submit per-

sonal data such as name, address, salary, age, and telephone number if they

(want) _____ to receive the discount card.

(5) When a clerk at the store asked me if I (want) _____

to sign up for a discount card, I said no. (6) I thought that if I provided the

store with personal data, they probably (sell) _____ it to a

marketing firm, and then I (7) (start) _____ to receive a lot of

junk mail and telemarketing calls. (8) The clerk said that the information

would not be sold, but if I (believe) _____ that, I wouldn't

have refused the card. (9) After all, if the company (not plan)

_____ to sell this information, why are they collecting it?

(10) A friend told me that she (fill out) _____ a form for
the discount card if she shopped at that store. (11) "They (use)
_____ information about your favorite products to target you
as a customer if you sign up," she said. (12) "Why not let them do that if you
(be) _____ already a customer of the store?"

(13) If I change my mind about the discount card, I (think)
_____ about filling out the form with false information. (14)
Even if I (be) _____ homeless, my friend told me, the store
would value my business. (15) "All people who shop there should be eligible
for the discounts, even if they (not have) _____ a home
address and telephone number," she said. (16) I (end up)
_____ visiting the drugstore as Jane Doe if I decide that my
friend is right.

Answers to the
Even-Numbered Exercises

NOUNS AND NOUN PHRASES

EXERCISE 64.1 Using count and noncount nouns

2. reasons
4. wealth
6. discrimination
8. Legislation
10. advice

EXERCISE 64.2 Revising errors in the use of count and noncount nouns

2. The idea that every person has a soul mate can build dangerously high *expectations*.
4. Young adults need to be realistic when they think about the *qualities* they want in a life partner.
6. A potential partner's suitability as a parent did not matter much to most people who took the survey.
8. The idea that a couple should have common beliefs about *religion* was also viewed as unimportant.
10. Perhaps too many young people are getting their *information* about marriage from television and romance novels instead of from real-life examples.

EXERCISE 64.3 Using singular and plural forms

2. ocean
4. corners
6. ports
8. diseases
10. officials

EXERCISE 64.4   Revising errors in the use of singular and plural forms

2. Four young *men* from Liverpool, England, made a fortune playing songs that young people everywhere loved.
4. Some buyers are middle-aged fans who have not lost any of the *respect* they had for the group in the 1960s.
6. Playing their favorite old pieces of *music* may make some fans feel young again.
8. Even today, a teenager is likely to have heard many bits of Beatle *trivia*.
10. The two surviving Beatles are in their early sixties, but their fans span all *ages*.

EXERCISE 64.6   Using determiners appropriately

2. a
4. X
6. their
8. a
10. this, America's

EXERCISE 64.7   Revising errors in the use of determiners

2. In fact, *a* person who cannot speak well in public is unlikely to be promoted to an executive position.
4. For these people, giving *a* speech is usually a miserable experience.
6. Taking *a* few deep breaths before a speech gives the speaker extra oxygen and can calm nerves.
8. When speakers remember something that made them laugh recently, *the* funny memory can help them to relax.
10. Many organizations can help to conquer a *businessperson's* fear of giving speeches.

EXERCISE 64.8   Using articles appropriately

2. the
4. a
6. a
8. A
10. an

EXERCISE 64.9 Eliminating unnecessary articles

2. Correct
4. The U.S. Supreme Court declared school prayer unconstitutional about forty years ago.
6. Correct
8. However, teachers or other authority figures in a school may not legally lead prayers in class or at school functions.
10. But, the law does not permit the use of class time in public schools for group expression of a particular faith.

EXERCISE 64.10 Revising errors in the use of articles

2. Grouping all Hispanics together ignores *the* fact that Hispanic Americans come from many different countries and cultures.
4. Just as not every Irish American agrees on political issues, there is not *a* single issue that guarantees all Hispanics' approval.
6. A high percentage of Hispanic residents of the United States believe that governments should provide assistance to *the* poor.
8. However, many Hispanic Americans are in [*no article necessary*] agreement with conservative political opinions about social issues.
10. His tactic may or may not have had *an* effect on Hispanic approval of his positions, for Hispanics in this country also disagree about the politics of speaking Spanish.

EXERCISE 64.11 Arranging modifiers appropriately

SUGGESTED ANSWERS

2. All these symptoms affect performance in certain jobs.
4. Nowadays, new research and openness about the condition help prevent potential job discrimination.
6. For an adult with A.D.D., such a task is a huge cognitive burden.
8. Organizing paperwork by color and size clears up some kinds of confusion for A.D.D. sufferers.
10. If it is not possible for them to change confusing daily office routines, A.D.D. sufferers should consider changing careers.

VERBS AND VERB PHRASES

EXERCISE 65.1   Using verb phrases

  2. learned
  4. are trying
  6. involve
  8. believe
10. united

EXERCISE 65.2   Revising verb phrases

SUGGESTED ANSWERS

  2. Those students who *have studied* formal written English may find conversational English difficult to understand.

  4. Conversation classes in English *are supposed* to help students become familiar with spoken English by simulating real-life situational dialogues.

  6. Just listening to spoken English *can be useful* in learning oral speech patterns and intonation.

  8. Some students who *do* not *feel* a need to learn spoken English might prefer to listen to radio broadcasts in their native language rather than broadcasts in English.

10. Students in English classes who *may* not *have been working* hard on learning spoken English need to understand that an inability to speak and understand English can limit their opportunities.

EXERCISE 65.3   Making subjects and verbs agree

Subjects are set in *italics,* verbs are set in **boldface.**

  2. A *man and* his nine-year-old *daughter* **were posing** next to a bison at Yellowstone when the bison butted the girl, according to a park spokesperson.

  4. *Each* of these examples **shows** that people take excessive risks in parks.

  6. The two *ideas* emphasized in the Grand Canyon's current safety campaign **are** that people should eat and drink regularly while on the trails and that they should avoid hiking during the heat of the day.

  8. Nevada's Lake Mead Recreation Area is one of the many *national parks* that **are banning** alcohol in order to reduce risky behavior on the part of visitors.

10. The *desire* for good photographs **is** one of the main reasons people forget to be cautious.

EXERCISE 65.4   Using the present and past tenses

2. remember
4. was
6. repeated
8. graduated
10. take

EXERCISE 65.5   Revising errors in the present and past tenses

2. My teacher *spent* the whole spring of 1996 drilling us on the practice tests.
4. Instead, they said that our school and the teachers *were* being tested.
6. My friend Hector said, "The test results *are* going to be sent to our parents."
8. I *scored* in the fiftieth percentile, so my results were exactly average.
10. I still believe that kids *learn* more in school when less time is spent on test preparation.

EXERCISE 65.7   Revising simple, perfect, and progressive verb phrases

SUGGESTED ANSWERS

2. The case of Central High School in Little Rock, Arkansas, *is* one of the most famous examples of a state fighting this federal mandate.
4. President Dwight D. Eisenhower ordered the army into Little Rock to enforce the court order, and African American children finally *entered* the school with the protection of federal troops.
6. However, over the years the courts *have* consistently *ruled* in favor of desegregation.
8. Recent statistics *show* that about 35 percent of African American students go to schools in which 90 percent of the student body is non-white.
10. Today, the fight for desegregation *has been* largely *replaced* by the fight for quality education for all students.

EXERCISE 65.8   Using modals appropriately

2. can
4. can
6. should
8. would
10. Will

EXERCISE 65.9   Revising errors in modal use

2.   I *couldn't* decide what career field interested me most, so selecting a major was difficult.

4.   My adviser told me that I *could* change my mind later if I decided I wasn't happy with my decision.

6.   When I took my first engineering course, I discovered that I *couldn't* understand some of the math required to complete my homework assignments.

8.   Now I am taking an extra math course to catch up, and I *will* finish my engineering degree next spring.

OR

Now I am taking an extra math course to catch up, and I *should* finish my engineering degree next spring.

10.   In the meantime, my professors tell me that I *should* study diligently to prepare for my career.

EXERCISE 65.10   Choosing appropriate modals

SUGGESTED ANSWERS

2.   had to struggle

4.   would have stayed (OR might have stayed)

6.   can enjoy (OR will enjoy)

8.   would feel (OR might feel)

10.   will prepare (OR can prepare)

EXERCISE 65.11   Using participial adjectives

2.   soothing

4.   tired

6.   shaking

8.   horrifying

10.   surprised

EXERCISE 65.12   Revising errors in the use of participial adjectives

2.   Correct

4.   However, *disgusted* patients soon tire of having amateurs use them to practice starting IVs, drawing blood, and giving injections.

6.   Correct

8.   The gagging sound is *unnerving*, but students' mistakes do not hurt any living human beings.

10. When these teaching techniques become more widespread, hospitalized people all over the United States will be *relieved*.

PREPOSITIONS AND PREPOSITIONAL PHRASES

EXERCISE 66.1   Using prepositions appropriately

2. of
4. with
6. in
8. to
10. about

EXERCISE 66.2   Revising inappropriate prepositions

2. *In* such situations, the workplace can provide a place for teens to interact with adult role models.
4. While they are in high school, students spend a lot of time *with* their friends or in class.
6. Working also gives students something to do *in* (OR *during*) the hours after school.
8. A part-time job can allow teens to pay *for* leisure activities that they would otherwise be unable to afford.
10. A teenager's ability to succeed both as a student and as a worker depends largely *on* his or her sense of responsibility.

EXERCISE 66.3   Using two-word verbs

2. from
4. to
6. at
8. to
10. to

EXERCISE 66.4   Revising errors in the use of two-word verbs

2. I looked *at* the course syllabus while she talked.
4. Neither would she cater *to* the whims of individual students, she added.
6. She then turned *from* her discussion of the syllabus to tell an anecdote from her teaching experiences.

8. She further encouraged us to invest *in* our education by developing good study habits for all our classes.

10. I concluded *from* her discussion that she wanted to be sure students would take her class seriously.

CLAUSES AND SENTENCES

EXERCISE 67.1   Choosing appropriate subjects

2. It
4. it
6. it
8. There
10. there

EXERCISE 67.2   Revising for appropriate verb placement

2. Most parents would *like* to monitor their children's television viewing.
4. One solution might *come* from recent technological innovations.
6. The *V stands* for "violence."
8. Parents *program* the chip to block shows with certain ratings.
10. Of course, today, many children *know* better than their parents how to program electronic devices.

EXERCISE 67.3   Revising for English word order

SUGGESTED ANSWERS

2. The ratings system is similar to the one used for movies.
4. Older children might be attracted to programming rated as explicit.
6. Parents with an older television will not be able to block out shows rated for mature audiences.
8. Advertisers worry that parents will block out the prime-time shows that generate the most advertising revenue.
10. The television industry argues that the V-chip is a kind of censorship since it will indirectly control the kinds of shows produced.

EXERCISE 67.4   Identifying noun clauses

2. How companies can help executives to cope when they return is an even more serious problem. *subject clause*
4. A study reveals that 25 percent of returning employees leave their companies within a year. *object clause*

6. <u>That so much money is at stake</u> motivates top managers to investigate the reasons for employee dissatisfaction. *subject clause*

8. Many returning executives complain <u>that their companies didn't tell them exactly what they would be working on when they returned.</u> *object clause*

10. <u>How companies will address these repatriation issues</u> is a challenge for today's business world. *subject clause*

EXERCISE 67.5   Using noun clauses

SUGGESTED ANSWERS

2. It is mandatory that these two pieces not exceed certain size requirements.

4. Travelers had to hand over as checked luggage whichever bags exceeded size restrictions.

6. In addition, it often upset busy business travelers' schedules whenever checked bags took a long time to arrive at the baggage claim.

8. Major airlines have suggested that airplanes increase the amount of space available in overhead bins so that passengers can bring more and larger carry-ons.

10. It is uncertain whether flight attendants will be happy about this change.

EXERCISE 67.6   Revising errors in noun clauses

SUGGESTED ANSWERS

2. Systems administrators can use software to see the amount of email that employees send and receive each day.

4. It could be considered a breach of privacy when managers read employees' email.

6. The systems administrator tells employees that it is his job to prevent problems.

8. It is true that companies have to buy more bandwidth if their employees send huge amounts of email.

10. It is important that managers create an atmosphere that makes employees feel trusted and fairly treated.

EXERCISE 67.8   Using infinitives and gerunds appropriately

2. to share

4. plagiarizing

6. to do

8. working

10. angering

EXERCISE 67.9   Revising errors in infinitives and gerunds

2.   International students who expect *to cooperate* with classmates may initially feel uncomfortable with the competition in American schools.

4.   In some courses, however, the instructor might decide *to calculate* students' grades in relation to one another.

6.   When a curve is used, students may be reluctant *to share* their lecture notes with others because they don't want to hurt their own grades.

8.   Employers trying to fill a job opening may also choose *to look* at a candidate's grade-point average and faculty recommendations.

10.   International students sometimes have to get used to *functioning* in this competitive system.

EXERCISE 67.10   Forming adjective clauses

SUGGESTED ANSWERS

2.   However, more often the teenager is the one who convinces the parent to pay for procedures.

4.   Media images of young men and women to which teens are frequently exposed show impossibly perfect faces and bodies.

   Teens are frequently exposed to media images of young men and women that show impossibly perfect faces and bodies.

6.   Therefore, people whose bodies aren't even fully developed are requesting plastic surgery.

8.   She demanded to have the wrinkles that were around her eyes removed.

10.   The problems, which prevented her from having the surgery, were that she was nineteen and that she had no wrinkles.

   The problems, which were that she was nineteen and that she had no wrinkles, prevented her from having the surgery.

EXERCISE 67.11   Revising errors in the use of relative pronouns in adjective clauses

2.   that; Correct

4.   whom; For instance, a musician with tattoos might not stand out, but a dentist with tattoos might be someone patients become nervous about.

6.   which; Removing a tattoo one no longer feels comfortable with is sometimes just a sign of moving on to a new stage in life.

8.   which; Correct

10.   which; Correct

EXERCISE 67.13   Selecting appropriate verb forms in conditional sentences

2. not watch
4. were
6. are
8. turn
10. becomes

EXERCISE 67.14   Using appropriate verb forms in conditional sentences

SUGGESTED ANSWERS

2. receive (OR will receive)
4. want
6. would sell
8. had believed
10. would have filled out
12. are
14. were
16. may end up